I Am...

Whole...

Healed...

Complete...

Forgiven...

Victorious...

Uniquely Created...

Enough...

Loved...

Royal...

Free...

Ashamed No More

ASHAMED NO MORE
Free At Last...Free At Last

Ashamed No More

To: _____

It is for freedom that Christ has set us free. Stand firm, then, and do not let yourselves be burdened again by a yoke of slavery. Galatians 5:1(NIV)

Copyright 2019, ©2024
by Renee Minor Johnson
ChampionsWithin Kingdom Builders
Publishing Company

All rights reserved. No part of the material protected by this copyright notice may be reproduced or utilized in any form or by any means, without the written permission of the author, except by a reviewer who may quote brief passages in a review. This includes, electronically or mechanically, photocopying/recording, or by any information storage and retrieval system.

ISBN: 978-0578452036
ChampionsWithin Kingdom Builders
Email: Championswithin2@yahoo.com
Website: www.royaltyjrenee.com

Scripture quotations marked (AMP) are taken from the Amplified Bible, Copyright © 1954, 1958, 1962, 1964, 1965, 1987 by The Lockman Foundation. Used by permission.

Scripture quotations marked (TPT) are from The Passion Translation®. Copyright © 2017, 2018 by Passion & Fire Ministries, Inc. Used by permission. All rights reserved. ThePassionTranslation.com.

The World English Bible is in the Public Domain. That means that it is not copyrighted. However, "World English Bible" is a Trademark.

"Scripture quotations noted CEB are taken from the Common English Bible, copyright 2011. Used by permission. All rights reserved."

Holy Bible, New Living Translation, copyright © 1996, 2004, 2007, 2013, 2015 by Tyndale House Foundation. Used by permission of Tyndale House Publishers Inc., Carol Stream, Illinois 60188. All rights reserved.

Scripture taken from The Message. Copyright © 1993, 1994, 1995, 1996, 2000, 2001, 2002. Used by permission of NavPress Publishing Group.

THE HOLY BIBLE, NEW INTERNATIONAL VERSION®, (NIV)® Copyright © 1973, 1978, 1984, 2011 by Biblica, Inc.™ Used by permission. All rights reserved worldwide.

Scripture quotations taken from the 21st Century King James Version®, copyright © 1994. Used by permission of Deuel Enterprises, Inc., Gary, SD 57237. All rights reserved.

GOD'S WORD is a copyrighted work of God's Word to the Nations. Quotations are used by permission. Copyright 1995 by God's Word to the Nations. All rights reserved.

Editors: Amanda Gail Simmons
Cover Design: Exodus 35 Designs and
                          Images by D. Marie
Cover Photo: Haylie Noel Photography

TABLE OF CONTENTS

Introduction............... ix

CHAPTER 1_____THE TOXICITY OF SHAME.................15

Chapter 2_____FEAR, FRET, & REGRET....................25

Chapter 3_____THE WEIGHT OF SHAME.................39

Chapter 4_____SHATTERING SHAME..........................53

Chapter 5_____DROP IT..63

Chapter 6_____A RENEWED MIND...............................75

Chapter 7_____YOUR TRUE IDENTITY......................87

Chapter 8_____KNOW YOUR WORTH.............................99

PAIN TO PASSION........................112

THE FAME OF HIS NAME...................113

*P*REFACE

Are guilt and shame the same? In my researching the difference between the two, I found that guilt is about doing wrong, and shame is about being wrong. The sense of **being wrong** *seems to follow misfortunes or mistakes; at some point, feelings of not being enough, being unlovable, and being unworthy can begin to take root. As you can see, neither of the above emotions is a true expression of our God-given identity. It is in God's love that we find our worth, our true identity, and our* **FREEDOM**.

Though guilt and shame are different by definition, the enemy uses them simultaneously in hopes of holding us captive by creating life altering distractions. I witnessed a quote that read, "Distraction is destruction in slow motion." After reading the quote, I had a visual image of how I previously allowed guilt and shame to move me slowly toward destruction. I was basically settling for less than God intended because I felt that is what I deserved.

*"***Ashamed No More***" is the roadmap of my testimonial journey of hills and valleys. I pray that as you read my story, you will be encouraged, uplifted, and released to walk in the authoritative power promised to us as children of the Most High God. Receive this book as your permission slip to experience a new level of* **FREEDOM**...
It belongs to you!!

*I*NTRODUCTION

"No longer imprisoned or entrapped by my past, or opinions of negative people that pass. Their words can't hold me, and their comments won't mold me."

The introductory quote is from the poem, "I Am a Queen." The poem is my story… my life's narrative. Each time I recite this poem, I experience a tangible form of freedom… freedom that can only be embraced when one refuses to look back. It's the type of freedom that disallows the past to negatively define the future. I believe that the ghost of our past can root us in a place of shame. I was told once that looking back can cause us to become frozen or entrapped in the posture of our past. In other words, ruminating over our mistakes, mishaps, or misfortunes can lead to becoming "stuck" in a cyclical pattern. I call it the place of "if I coulda, woulda, shoulda." Moving forward requires looking forward. There is no safety, or success, in driving forward while looking backward.

At the age of 14, I was in a near-fatal car wreck with my oldest sister and her family. As a result of the accident, I experienced a significant amount of trauma to my left leg. Due to the injuries, multiple surgeries were required. The scarring from the injuries and the surgeries was very noticeable. As a teenager, I was very self-conscious about my summer wardrobe due to my scars. My comfort zone was knee shorts, and sundresses. Clearly, God had granted me a second chance at life, but I was hiding the evidence! It was a blessing to come out of the accident alive, and have both legs. Instead of sharing the testimony of how God rescued me from the jaws of death, I hid in shame. I didn't realize that the scarring that started on the outside, began to make its way to the inside. Shame was starting to grow and fester like cancer. Does that sound familiar? Though it took me a while to grasp, I finally realized that the very thing that God wanted to use as a TESTIMONY, the enemy was trying to use as handcuffs. Fact says, "I have scars", but TRUTH says, "I have a testimony." Paul said (in 2 Timothy 1:8), "Don't be ashamed to testify about our Lord." Overcoming comes out of the testifying.

My journey has taken me up some mountains and into some valleys… on some straight roads and on some winding roads… roads I thought I'd never get off. It suddenly dawned on me that I was moving forward while looking back, and that was causing me to sink deeper and deeper into the abyss of shame. The "abyss of shame" can be caused by childhood traumas (such as feelings of rejection, abandonment, or abuse). I'm convinced that some traumatic experiences can cause cracks in our physical and spiritual foundation. When foundational cracks are not healed and sealed, fear, fret, and regret can turn the small openings into sinkholes with shame being the culprit of it all.

Healing the cracks created by guilt and shame begins with forgiveness. Forgiving ourselves and others is a primary component of experiencing freedom. It is the Holy Spirit that gives us the ability to embrace forgiveness and receive the liberating peace of God. Forgiveness along with peace and freedom, are eternal promises of God, and I am so grateful for His promises. True peace is birthed out of knowing our true identity. True freedom is birthed out of walking in the authority of our true identity. Simultaneously, peace and freedom are conceived in the presence of God; in this case, conception is a prerequisite for perception.

The time has come for us to perceive who we are in Christ and walk in the authority of our true identity. We are a chosen generation… a royal priesthood. I believe that as we embrace the revelation of the power and anointing connected to our priestly identity, we gain strength to push beyond the reality of our painful yesterdays. Walking in our true identity is essential in breaking through the barriers of shame. It is time to leave the past in the past and **live forward**. Now is the time to declare a new thing:

"I am free from the shadows of shame. No longer will I be shaken or shackled by my past mistakes, or misfortunes. I am forgiven and I am free. I know my worth; I am Royalty... and that's how He sees me. I call upon you Heavenly Father, to replace the spirit of fear, defeat, disgrace, sadness, regret, anxiety, and shame, with your unexplainable peace... your sufficient grace... and your unmerited favor." I decree and declare that the joy of the Lord is my strength!
In Jesus Name, Amen

So, if the Son sets you free, you will be free indeed.
John 8:36

CHAPTER 1
THE TOXICITY OF SHAME

Wikipedia defines shame as "a discrete, basic emotion that prompts people to hide or deny their wrongdoings." Have you ever felt the weight of shame pressing down on you, making you feel worthless or powerless, causing you to withdraw or hide? Shame is an unpleasant self-conscious emotion that distorts our sense of self-worth and leads to negative self-evaluation. In these moments, it can be difficult to recognize that such feelings do not reflect the character of our Almighty God. Everything shame represents was covered by the blood of Jesus, and there is nothing small or powerless about that.

The blood of Jesus covers everything that does not reflect Him... including shame. **Shame** is thought to derive from the Old English word *"hama"*, which means to veil or to cover. In other words, the Blood of Jesus "covers the cover."

The toxicity of shame can be paralyzing. It is deceptive in nature as it poses as a means of being a safe hiding place. Well, let me tell you this, there is nothing safe about shame. As a matter of fact, my description of shame is more like a flesh-eating parasite; you can't see the attack, but it's there. It lies underneath the skin eating away everything pertaining to "life." Whenever one begins to believe they are what they did, or they are what happen to them, the parasite of shame is near. My prayer is that you will not allow the poison of shame to taint any area of your life. Remove the stopper, and "drain the paralyzing toxicity of shame."

Free Indeed

As human beings, all of us are guilty of doing, saying, or thinking of things that we aren't proud to admit... things that left us feeling "ashamed." With that being said, I have joy knowing that even in our wrongdoing, God's love for us never changes. It took me decades to grasp the revelation that we serve a loving and forgiving God. He carried shame to the grave and left it there; it is not His will that we bring it back to life. Matthew 18:18 says, "Truly I tell you, whatever you bind on earth will be bound in heaven, and whatever you loose on earth will be loosed in heaven." I eventually found peace in knowing, in my knower, that He who the Son has set free is indeed free... that includes me!!

John 1:3 says that nothing exists apart from God... (That means no-thing... no healing, no freedom, no peace, and no strength) absolutely nothing. Our relationship with God is essential for our freedom; our relationship with God is essential for breaking through the barriers of shame. While navigating through the challenges of life, I learned to use my past to sharpen me; this concept has been life changing. In the midst of the challenges I realized that it wasn't my past blocking me, "it was me, blocking me." Many times, the enemy was **"the inner me."** Flesh and blood did not reveal that to me; the Holy Spirit downloaded that revelation.

Trusting my head-knowledge for deliverance was a total disaster. The toxicity of shame was making me bitter... not better. My deliverance did not come through self-esteem or self-confidence (neither of those things have power). My deliverance evolved with me trusting God; my God-confidence has unlimited power. I can do all things through Christ who gives me strength. His strength is sufficient for all experiences, even those that may seem more traumatic than others.

The Bible teaches that true growth after trauma is possible when we rely on God's sufficient grace rather than our own strength (2 Corinthians 1:8-11). Studies have shown that people can become stronger and experience positive growth following trauma. The UNC-Charlotte/PTG Research Group refers to this as "Posttraumatic Growth." On my personal Damascus Road, I experienced this growth when I made a conscious shift in my focus, turning towards God's promises rather than my circumstances. This transformation... this newfound hope and inspiration, is something I'm deeply thankful to Daddy-God for. It was a true awakening that helped me understand how to realign my vision, allowing me to let go of my own efforts and truly grow in God. The caveat here is this..."Growing in God requires a shift... a shift in focus, mental attitude, and commitment... This combination will bring change, and eventually break chains." I strongly believe that our attentiveness to our directional focus can play a major part in our spiritual growth (or the lack thereof).

"With everything that has happened to you, you can either feel sorry for yourself or treat what has happened as a gift. Everything is either an opportunity to grow or an obstacle to keep you from growing. You get to choose."
~Wayne W. Dyer

All this is proceeding along lines planned all along by God and then executed in Christ Jesus. When we trust in him, we're free to say whatever needs to be said, bold to go wherever we need to go. So don't let my present trouble on your behalf get you down. Be proud!
Ephesians 3:12-13(MSG)

Trust in the Lord completely, and do not rely on your own opinions. With all your heart rely on him to guide you, and he will lead you in every decision you make. Become intimate with him in whatever you do, and he will lead you wherever you go.
Proverbs 3:5-6 (TPT)

So don't lose your confidence. It will bring you a great reward. 36 You need endurance so that after you have done what God wants you to do, you can receive what he has promised.
Hebrews 10:35-36(GW)

Consider it a sheer gift, friends, when tests and challenges come at you from all sides. You know that under pressure, your faith-life is forced into the open and shows its true colors. So don't try to get out of anything prematurely. Let it do its work so you become mature and well-developed, not deficient in any way.
James 1:2-4(MSG)

Whenever our hearts make us feel guilty and remind us of our failures, we know that God is much greater and more merciful than our conscience, and he knows everything there is to know about us.
1 John 3:20 (TPT)

We learn from yesterday when we leave it... not live in it!!

What are your takeaways from this chapter?

MY FREEDOM PRAYER

_____
_____
_____
_____
_____
_____
_____
_____
_____
_____
_____
_____
_____
_____
_____
_____

ASHAMED NO MORE
Free at last...Free at last

Abba Father...

The one who
embraces the embarrassed,
and
the one who is the healer of pain,
is the one who calms
my doubts and my fears...
He's the one
who
freed me from shame!!
-RMJ

CHAPTER 2
*F*EAR, *F*RET, & *R*EGRET

"Fear and regret have one thing in common—both are based on events that don't exist in the present time."
~Joleen Lee

When the emotion of "fret" is added to fear and regret, the combination can create a paralyzing toxin; it's called **shame**. Allow me to go deeper. It is possible to become frozen in the position of our past when **fear** (afraid of people finding out about our past), **fret** (nervous, anxious, and worried about what people will think of us when they find out about our past), and **regret** (ruminating on the mistakes of our past in the Rolodex of our mind day after day) is present. In the form of an equation, I would say that fear+ fret+ regret= "shame."

In my new-found hobby of gardening, I realized that it is necessary to have the proper soil and herbicide for healthy growth. The importance of the herbicide is to kill overpowering, smothering weeds. After applying the chemical to the designated areas, I noticed the wilting away of the unwanted weeds. At that point I had a revelation; just as weeds can overtake and kill the growth of a healthy garden, shame has the potential of doing the same in our lives. Shame contains dream killing, hope stealing, toxins that block the forthcoming of purpose. It is invisible in nature, yet it has a suffocating presence which acts as a roadblock on our journey to our predetermined destiny assignments.

About 35 years ago, fear, fret, and regret was a smothering cloud that hovered over my head. Imagine this scenario... an eighteen year old girl, youngest daughter of a pastor, just out of high school, the first year of college..."Pregnant." Yep, that's right... pregnant. This scenario was my "truth" and I carried the emotions attached to fear, fret and regret for many years. The equation of it all equaled shame in my world.

I believe that shame is one of the enemy's most conniving weapons. It is a weighted-dagger that contradicts the promises of God. The enemy uses the dagger of shame to distort how we see ourselves. His ultimate goal is to make us feel unworthy of walking in our God-given purpose. Our defense for the enemy's weapons, is God's promises… "No weapon formed against us shall prosper." At the age of eighteen, I didn't have the full revelation of God's promises, and I was tormented in my mind for a very long time. Fear, fret, and regret poisoned my mind with the mistakes and mishaps of my past in an attempt to taint my future. I carried the baggage of shame for many years, and I know the heaviness of it all too well… but God. Underneath the weight of it all, I remember hearing a still small voice, "I, the Lord, am your light and your salvation, whom shall you fear… I am your strength… no need to be afraid."

Some might believe that fret and fear are one and the same. However, as I researched the definition of the word fret this is what I found: **Fret:** to be nervous, anxious, or worried. Another definition says "to fret is to express anxiety or worry, annoyance, or to be discontent." When you *fret* over something, it consumes your thoughts. The word "fret" is related to the word friction. Friction causes destructive heat; it wears away, irritates, and annoys. This definition resonated with my spirit. I experienced anxiety and worry that gradually burned away, irritated, and annoyed my faith, my hopes, and my dreams, and again I say, "but God." His word stands when everything else seems to fade.

Philippians 4:6-7 (MSG) says, "Don't fret or worry. Instead of worrying, pray. Let petitions and praises shape your worries into prayers, letting God know your concerns. Before you know it, a sense of God's wholeness, everything coming together for good, will come and settle you down. It's wonderful what happens when Christ displaces worry at the center of your life." Just as fear, fret, and regret lead to shame, praise, prayer, and gratitude lead to peace. It's not merely the promises of God that lift the weight of shame—it's having faith in those promises. My faith was pivotal in breaking the chains of shame. I am no longer a slave to fear, fret, and regret; I am a praising, praying child of God.

The same spirit that resurrected Jesus from the grave is alive in us as believers. We have been given the power to rise up from the tomb of our past. The stone of "shame" has been rolled away. Freedom belongs to us. He who the Son sets free is indeed FREE!!

Often times we view our past as an obstacle blocking us from our future, but I beg to differ. I've learned that the thing the enemy used to hold me down is the very thing that gave me the grit and tenacity to "fight forward." It is the "forward fight" that leads us into VICTORY!! 2 Corinthians 2:14 says, "In Christ, God leads us from place to place in one perpetual victory parade."

As we grow daily, in the knowledge of Christ, we should declare victory over every situation. The declaration is not based on what we see... it's based on God's promise. In other words, there is no opposition greater than God's power, purpose or promise. Matter of fact, God knows how to make opposition work in our favor; it can bring strength to our spiritual muscles when we press forward and upward. With that being said, keep pressing; freedom belongs to you. What's ahead of you is far greater than what is behind you.

My path to freedom was in my God-given ability to choose. I had to decide if I was going to live inside or outside of **my personal** prison of shame; I chose to break free. I changed my focus and used opposition as an opportunity to rise. Despite the fact that it took years to get this revelation, I was making progress. I started looking at things differently... I started thinking differently. When you're get tired of hearing the same sad song over and over, what do you do? You change the station, right? Well, that's what I did. Instead of ruminating on my disappointment (due to being pregnant at the age of eighteen without a husband), I changed stations. I finally realized that God's assignment for my life didn't change with my mess-ups. God has no problem mastering our mess-ups. Thank God that our promised purpose is much greater than our past mistakes.

I am fully convinced that every intrinsic detail of our lives is woven together to fit into God's perfect plan. His plans for us include good (not harm), peace, hope, and a prosperous future.

*Satan loves to take what's beautiful and ruin it.
God loves to take what's ruined and make it
beautiful.
~Priscilla Shirer*

Who is…..

The filler of every void…
The healer of every heart…
The lifter of every bowed down head,
and mender of broken parts.
His resurrection POWER made
available to you and me,
is the power that broke the chains of
shame…
It's the POWER that SET US FREE!!

"His Name is… JESUS"

~RMJ

The Lord is my revelation-light to guide me along the way, he's the source of my salvation to defend me every day. I fear no one! I'll never turn back and run from you, Lord; surround and protect me.2 When evil ones come to destroy me, they will be the ones who turn back.3 My heart will not be afraid even if an army rises to attack. I know that you are there for me, so I will not be shaken. Psalm 27:1-3 (TPT)

"I sought the Lord, and he answered me and delivered me from all my fears. Those who look to him are radiant, and their faces shall never be ashamed."
Psalm 34:4-5(NIV)

Don't fear, because I am with you; don't be afraid, for I am your God. I will strengthen you, I will surely help you; I will hold you with my righteous strong hand.
Isaiah 41:10 (CEB)

Therefore if anyone is in Christ [that is, grafted in, joined to Him by faith in Him as Savior], he is a new creature [reborn and renewed by the Holy Spirit]; the old things
[the previous moral and spiritual condition] have passed away. Behold, new things have come [because spiritual awakening brings a new life].
2 Corinthians 5:17 (AMP)

So now the case is closed. There remains no accusing voice of condemnation against those who are joined in life-union with Jesus, the Anointed One.
Romans 1:8 (TPT)

Has there been a season (or more than one) of your life that was filled with fear, fret, and regret?

_____

_____

How did you handle the weight of it all?

_____

_____

_____

_____

_____

_____

How would you handle it differently today?

_____

_____

_____

_____

_____

_____

_____

_____

_____

MY FREEDOM PRAYER

_____
_____
_____
_____
_____
_____
_____
_____
_____
_____
_____
_____
_____
_____

ASHAMED NO MORE
Free at last...Free at last

> "Never be defined by your past. It was just a lesson, not a life sentence."
> —Unknown

We can freely release the weight of shame when we trust in the Lord to take care of us.

~~~~~~~~~~~~~~~~~~~~~~~~~~

Trust in the Lord with you whole heart... Proverbs 3:5

CHAPTER 3
THE WEIGHT OF SHAME

The weighted shackles of shame, portrayed in many forms, can lead to an identity crisis. Targeting our identity is just one of the enemy's many tactics in attacking our witness for God. He uses the weight of shame as a vice to keep us at bay from our divine destiny. He uses our past as an entrance into our future. His stealthy whispers of negativity say, "You've done too much bad to amount to anything good." He spews his poisonous lies to bruise our identity; he wants to minimize our effectiveness in our Kingdom purpose. Although he can't have our inheritance, he can tarnish our perception of the power and authority we have as "The King's Kids."

Webster's dictionary defines shame as a feeling of guilt, regret, or sadness that you have because you know you have done something wrong; a feeling of guilt, regret, or embarrassment, dishonor or disgrace. Although Webster didn't mention fear or unforgiveness in the definition, I believe that both emotions magnetically connect to shame. Fear and unforgiveness (toward us and others) can cause the weight of shame to become "**ultra-heavy**."

Fear caused Adam and Eve to hide from God in the garden after they disobeyed His command. Once their eyes were open to sin, they were ashamed and they covered themselves. It reminds me of going through the potty-training stages with my children. Whenever they didn't quite make it to the potty, and needed to be cleaned, I would find them hiding. In disappointment and fear, they would hide in the corner. Wouldn't it be a sad and smelly situation if they carried the stench of fear, embarrassment, and regret all-day every day? I believe that this analogy describes our behavior when we fall short, and allow the weight of shame to hold us back from God's promises. We're just like infants; they can't successfully clean themselves and neither can we!!

Many times we go through life carrying a weight of shame, and we fail to realize it. We avoid people, defer opportunities, and dumb-down God-given abilities due to shame. Yes... I believe shame is the culprit. I am totally convinced that the enemy uses this weight to hold us from our destiny. Hebrews 12:1 encourages us to lay aside every weight, and the sin that can beset, oppress, or afflict us. One translation says, "Let's throw off any extra baggage, and get rid of the sin that trips us up." In other words, throw off the shame and the sin that weighs us down. It's time to lay it down and move forward.

Have you ever spoken negative statements like, "I can't do that, I'm not good enough, not smart enough, not holy enough, I'm too old, they won't listen to me?" Most times, these words are birthed out of feeling less than (due to past experiences). I would go a step further and say that some hurt may have been "church hurt" **(but that's another book-smile)**. All in all, I believe statements of inferiority arise when we are unaware of our worth.

The plot of the enemy is to use our past missteps as a dis-qualifier; he will set up a smoke screen to make us believe that we've missed the mark... but God. What the enemy doesn't understand is that Romans 8:28 (TPT) qualifies us... regardless of our mishaps and hiccups. The scripture says, "So we are convinced that every detail of our lives is continually woven together to fit into God's perfect plan of bringing good into our lives, for we are his lovers who have been called to fulfill his designed purpose." To God be the Glory; what the devil meant for evil, God used it for our good. We have the victory over the enemy, and this victory empowers us in our journey.

I can list names of imperfect people in the Bible used to accomplish God's will. Allow me to name a few:

Noah, a Drunkard; **Moses**, a Stutterer; **David**, a Murderer and Adulterer; **Rahab**, a Prostitute; **Saul**(before he became Paul), a Christian killer; and the Samaritan Woman, five Husbands and a live-in (ha-ha-ha). All of them had different thorns, but there is one thing they had in common, they were all recipients of God's universal grace. God's purpose for our lives doesn't change due to our imperfections. He will work it all together for good. His grace is sufficient for all.

Just like Noah, Moses, David, Rahab, Saul, and the Samaritan Woman, I discovered that my mistakes didn't disqualify me from God's purpose. Each of them had flaws, yet God used their brokenness for His glory. Their stories remind us that our imperfections don't cancel God's plans; instead, they become the very places where His grace shines the brightest.

Through the Eyes of Grace

When God decided to save us from destruction, our imperfections had no bearing on His decision. He said, "If any man/woman be **in Christ** we are made new." It is so good to know that God's grace is not determined by the size of our mess: however, our ability to receive it is determined by our faith. I am grateful for the revelation that I am saved by grace… not by performance. Ephesians 2:8 says, "For it is by grace you have been saved, through faith and it is not from yourselves, it is the gift of God." Grace is defined as, "The freely given, unmerited favor and love of God; the influence or spirit of God operating in humans to regenerate or strengthen them." Remember, we are saved by grace through faith.

Grace is a gift given by the Almighty God… to his royal children. As believers, grace and royalty are part of our inheritance, yet they both come with responsibility. Grace is more than unmerited favor. It is more than the material blessings we receive that we don't deserve. It is not a permission slip to justify selfish desires and not live up to our full potential. God's grace saves, then it enlightens. It saves, and then it uplifts. It saves, empowers, and builds. Grace teaches us to do the right thing, and infused grace empowers us to do the job. Grace gives us the ability to walk according to God's divine purpose... enabling us to align our actions with a higher purpose, even when faced with challenges from our past. When the thorns of our missteps are still in place, God's grace is enough to overcome them and move forward.

Our royal position comes only through Father God; we are His sons and daughters. We are children of the King. Our royal position is not predicated on our ethnicity, family background, or economic status. We were adopted into the royal family, and our position hinges on God's "AMAZING GRACE." Once we discover that nothing can separate us from God's love, we can then live free from shame and the burden of living a "performance"based life. It is God's amazing grace and his inseparable love that brings freedom... freedom from shame produced from past abuse, painful rejection, fear, fret, and regret. His perfect love covers our fragile imperfections. I love the song "You Still Love Me" by Koryn Hawthorn. The lyrics are:

> *"See I'm not perfect, I don't deserve it*
> *You didn't change your mind, left my past behind, oh See I'm not perfect but still -you call me worthy,*
> *You didn't change your mind, left my past behind,*
> *You still love me, I know you still love me*
> *You still love me even when I fall."*

Although we are not perfect, we serve a perfect God who loves us perfectly. His perfect unconditional love promises to "lift up those who are bent over with burdens of shame." In spite of my missteps and mistakes that caused me to lose my balance, I'm grateful that God showed himself to be the great EQUALIZER in my life. His love brought balance to everything out of alignment. When we are filled with God's love, there is no room for fear and shame. 1 John 4:18 makes it clear... where God's love is present, fear (and all of its attachments) is not.

~~~~~~~~~~~~~~~~~~~~~~~~~~~~~~~~~~~~~

So we must let go of every wound that has pierced us and the sin we so easily fall into. Then we will be able to run life's marathon race with passion and determination, for the path has been already marked out before us.
Hebrews 12:1(TPT)

So don't lose a minute in building on what you've been given, complementing your basic faith with good character, spiritual understanding, alert discipline, passionate patience, reverent wonder, warm friendliness, and generous love, each dimension fitting into and developing the others. With these qualities active and growing in your lives, no grass will grow under your feet, no day will pass without its reward as you mature in your experience of our Master Jesus.
2 Peter 1:5-9 (MSG)

He is so rich in kindness and grace that he purchased our freedom with the blood of his Son and forgave our sins.
Ephesians 1:7 (NLT)

It will happen in that day, that his burden will depart from off your shoulder, and his yoke from off your neck, and the yoke shall be destroyed because of the anointing oil.
Isaiah 10:27(WEB)

**Weak and feeble ones you will sustain.
Those bent over with burdens of shame you will lift up.
Psalm 145:14 (TPT)**

**At that moment their eyes were opened, and they suddenly felt
shame at their nakedness. So they sewed fig leaves
together to cover themselves.
Genesis 3:7 (NLT)**

**"You didn't choose me, remember; I chose you, and put you in
the world to bear fruit, fruit that won't spoil. As fruit bearers,
whatever you ask the Father in relation to me, he gives you.
John 15:16 (MSG)**

What are your top two takeaways from this chapter and why?

_____
_____
_____
_____
_____
_____
_____
_____
_____
_____
_____

Do you want to be free? _____
What will you let go of to experience freedom?

_____
_____
_____
_____
_____
_____
_____
_____
_____
_____
_____
_____
_____
_____
_____
_____
_____
_____
_____
_____
_____
_____
_____
_____

MY FREEDOM PRAYER

_____

_____

_____

_____

_____

_____

_____

_____

_____

_____

_____

_____

_____

_____

_____

ASHAMED NO MORE
Free at last...Free at last

GET READY FOR BREAKTHROUGH...

"Fear not; you will no longer live in shame. Don't be afraid; there is no more disgrace for you. You will no longer remember the shame of your youth and the sorrows of widowhood."
Isaiah 54:4(NLT)

CHAPTER 4
SHATTERING SHAME

Jesus, the author, and finisher of our faith, endured the cross, despising shame...
Hebrew 12:2

Shame can sometimes leave us paralyzed or frozen in a state of fear. "What if they talk about me, what if they laugh at me, what if it doesn't work... sounds familiar? When fear follows shame, isolation and cover-up are right behind. Jesus ignored shame by refusing to fall prey to the distractions surrounding him. He ignored shame by staying focused on his God-given purpose and carrying out the mission set before him. Hebrew 12:2(AMP) makes it plain... "For the joy [of accomplishing the goal] set before Him endured the cross, disregarding the shame, and sat down at the right hand of the throne of God [revealing, His deity, His authority, and the completion of His work]." His faith in the promises of His Heavenly Father shattered shame. The Scripture lets us know that when we resist distractions and keep our focus on the promises of God, **we** can shatter shame as well. When we believe, and stand firm on the TRUTH of God's Word (He is who He says He is, and He will do what He says He will do) we will shatter shame and rise up victoriously.

Shame is commonly defined as an intense negative emotion characterized by the perception of a global devaluation of self. This emotion is often triggered by social events, such as a drop of personal status or feelings of rejection, which can deeply affect individuals. According to an article by the Association of Psychological Science, shame is the powerful desire to hide away. People who are experiencing shame typically avoid others. As I read this particular study I was reminded of the "woman at the well." In her attempt to avoid others and isolate herself... her shame was shattered. Allow me to walk you through you through the journey of her "Well" experience.

According to John 4, the meeting between the Samaritan woman and Jesus was "atypical." This woman was of a race of people that the Jews despised. She was considered an outcast from the Jews perspective, but she was also an outcast among her own people. She was frowned upon by her own community, so she decided to go draw water from the well alone. The voices, the whispers, and chattering of those close to her were like a blanket of shame. I can imagine that in her mind, the alone place was a safe place. Allow me to enlighten you, it is in the "alone place" where isolation begins.

~~~~~~

"Self-forgiveness is the key that unlocks the chains of regret, allowing us to move forward with grace and embrace the healing that comes from letting go."

Forgiveness

The Samaritan woman, who had a past that was considered immoral, found herself face-to-face with Jesus. The Bible tells us that she had been married five times, and the man she was with at the time (number six) was not her husband. Her repeated patterns seemed to reflect a longing for connection and love, leading her to habitual actions. Both her emotional need for acceptance and her physical thirst for water were profoundly addressed in Jesus' presence. It was as though He dissected her heart, peeling back layers of lies and shame that had haunted her. In the presence of Grace, the illusion of who she thought she was dissolved, and the chains of her past were broken. At that moment, the transformative power of grace was evident as she forgave herself. Those who had judged her past witnessed her conversion unfold before their eyes.

It is God's grace and mercy that brings direction when we feel lost; grace opens our eyes in blindness. For the Samaritan, I truly believe that her "well experience" imparted the revelation that her past may have affected her, but it did not define her. Her freedom included self-forgiveness. Learning to forgive "me" was one of my greatest challenges.

A Message of Forgiveness

"You were doing the best you could at the time, given the resources apparent to you. As you journey through life and acquire a better understanding and awareness, typically, you look back on the past with a feeling of regret and remorse for your actions. What if, in looking back on your past, you did so with a compassionate heart filled with forgiveness rather than shame? Release the weight of carrying your past into your present. In doing so, you not only begin the healing process by simultaneously bringing new life to your today and your tomorrow. Make peace with your past."

Explore Your Feelings/Mission.

The Illusion

John 10:10 says, "The thief comes only to steal and kill and destroy; I have come that they may have life, and have it to the full." Though the first part of this scripture exposes the fact that the day we were born, traps were set up to deter us from coming into the full knowledge of our true identity. The second part of the scripture lets me know that I have a right to live an abundant life of freedom. Childhood trauma; mental, emotional, and physical abuse are just a few of the plots that the enemy uses to send us into a vortex of shame. Please understand this… the plots were set to create an illusion that we are what happened to us.

Along life's journey, all of the hurt, pain, betrayal, and rejection weighs us down… masking our TRUE IDENTITY. It's just an illusion. We are not what happened to us, and we are not what we did. We are who God called us. We are the royal Kings and Queens spoken of in Psalms 8:5. Many times we may not feel like royalty. When we look in the mirror, we don't see royalty; but, the truth of the matter is this, it's not about what we see, nor is it about our feelings. What

God called us is the only thing that matters. We are ROYALTY; that's what He called us and that's how He sees us.

I want you to know this, though you may have suffered mishaps and misfortunes, and those misfortunes and traumatic experiences were real, they did not **define** you. God's love defines and **refines** us. As we begin to walk in our true identity, it is necessary to stay connected to the one who gave us our identification. Every time the enemy makes an attempt to bring up your past and impart the weight of guilt and shame, begin to declare what God says about you. Begin to praise God for your true identity. Regardless of what you see, praise Him for what you believe to see... praise Him for the promises.

As children of God, we must always remember that shame is not a promise, nor a part of our DNA. Isaiah 63:1 says that we were given a garment of **praise** for the spirit of heaviness; that's a promise. Proclaim your true identity with confidence, praising God for what's to come. Turn your eyes to the Lord and declare His Word over your life. This act of declaring His Word is a powerful tool, for he promised that those who look to Him are radiant and their faces are never covered with shame (**Psalms 34:5**). Therefore, wash off your past, change your garment, and praise your way forward. Flee with swift feet from your yesterday and step into your tomorrow; this is your weapon for shattering shame. It is time to leave the past **BEHIND!!!**

~~~~~~~~~~~~~~~~~~~~~~~~~~~~~~~~~~~~

Yet You have made him a little lower than [a]God, And You have crowned him with glory and honor.
Psalm 8:5 (AMP)

If we claim that we're free of sin, we're only fooling ourselves. A claim like that is errant nonsense. On the other hand, if we admit our sins—make a clean breast of them—he won't let us down; he'll be true to himself. He'll forgive our sins and purge us of all wrongdoing.
1 John 1:8-9(MSG)

Forgetting the past and looking forward to what lies ahead, 14 I press on to reach the end of the race and receive the heavenly prize for which God, Through Christ Jesus, is calling us.
Philippians 3:13-14(NLT)

The woman then left her waterpot, and went her way into the city, and saith to the men, 29 Come, see a man, which told me all things that ever I did: is not this the Christ?
John 4:28-29 (KJV)

~~~~~~

- Make a list of the chains that you need to shatter in order for you to move forward.

_____
_____
_____
_____
_____
_____
_____
_____
_____
_____
_____
_____

MY FREEDOM PRAYER

ASHAMED NO MORE
Free at last...Free at last

CHAPTER 5
*D*ROP IT

*O*ur posture is easily affected or altered when we are weighed down with too much baggage. That would include physical bags (luggage, shopping) and spiritual bags (emotional issues). I am convinced that as sons and daughters of the King, there is a posture of confidence that lets the enemy know whose we are. When we drop the excess weight, we can then correct our royal posture. It is not the will of God for us to be crushed down with excessive burdens. Our ability to move forward, and upward, will be determined by the weight we are carrying. I'm not talking about physical weight; I'm talking about spiritual and emotional weight.

Let's talk about airplanes for a brief moment. There is a maximum weight requirement for all aircraft. The weight and balance requirements are put in place as a safety mechanism for effective aircraft performance. When the weight is over the recommended limit, it reduces flight performance, hinders the ability to maintain the proper altitude, and in many cases can lead to a fatal crash. Now, let's apply this same principle to our lives. The excess weight of carrying old, unnecessary baggage/ burdens will always hinder us from ascending to our assigned, divine destiny.

Let's talk about the woman at the well again. During her meeting with Jesus, she had two revelations. Her first revelation was how she saw Jesus and the second one was how she saw herself. Being in the presence of God changed her life by setting her free. She let go of her past, her sin, and her shame. The life she had lived before meeting Jesus could no longer remain. Upon her awakening, she "dropped her pot," her past, and her embarrassment, and shared her "Well

Experience" with everyone she met. Once again, here's another **"but God"** situation where the enemy's intentions failed. The Samaritan Woman was no longer held hostage... her misery became her ministry and her prison became her platform.

The future holds greater opportunities than the past. It's time to move forward. The burden you've been carrying is too heavy; it's filled with unforgiveness, lies, insecurities, fear, regret, and shame. If you want to achieve more in the latter part of your life, you must release the first half. This reminds me of an very inspiring fictional story titled, **"The Rebirth of an Eagle."**

> There an Eagle that was told it could live up to 70 years. But, to reach this age, the eagle must make a hard decision. In its 40th year, its long and flexible talons can no longer grab prey which serves as food; its long and sharp beak becomes bent. It's old-aged and heavy wings, due to their thick feathers, stick to its chest & make it difficult to fly. So, the eagle is left with two options: DIE or go through a painful process of CHANGE which could last up to 150 days. The process required that the eagle flies to a mountain top and sit on its nest. There the eagle knocks its beak against a rock until it plucks it out. Then the eagle would have to wait for a new beak to grow back; then it will pluck out its talons. When its new talons grow back, the eagle starts plucking its old-aged feathers. After about 5 months, the eagle would take its famous flight of rebirth and live for 30 more years. Many times, in order to survive, it is a "must" that we change!

What a profound message. We will never be able to rise above opposition unless we are willing to go through the process of letting go of the old. When this happens, our latter can truly be greater than the former. Lay aside the weight... the shame... that's distancing you from your divine destiny. Make a decision today that you will not allow the tears of your past to smother the fire of your future. Don't allow the weight shame to steal your true destiny.

It's Time to Let Go

One powerful strategy for letting go of the pain of the past is to rewrite key aspects of our story from a more balanced perspective. Simply put, we are our story. It's not always about the story of the events in our lives... it's the story we tell ourselves over and over again. I call it "pain on repeat." I believe that healthy rewrite including God's promises invites the mindset of a "victor" (as opposed to a victim).

Letting go of old attachments and soul-ties open up new opportunities and possibilities. Letting go means to pull down old, unproductive, thought patterns... it means facing up to your fears and then calling on your courage and your character to stare it down. It's not easy, but it's necessary. Replacing my old, unproductive, thought patterns with the mind- renewing Word of God, changed the trajectory of my life. The life application of the Word reduced the magnitude of my past from a mountain to an anthill. It wasn't my own strength that guided my Damascus road experience; it was the hand of God. I had to forget my past as I fastened my heart to my future.

The message of redemption, hope, and abundant life was prophesied throughout the Bible; from the Old Testament to the New Testament. Micah 7:18-2 (MSG) says, "Where is the god[small **g**] who can compare with you—wiping the slate clean of guilt, turning a blind eye, a deaf ear, to the past sins of your purged and precious people? You don't nurse your anger and don't stay angry long, for mercy is your specialty. That's what you love most. And compassion is on its way to us. You'll stamp out our wrongdoing. You'll sink our sins to the bottom of the ocean. You'll stay true to your word to Father Jacob and continue the compassion you showed Grandfather Abraham— everything you promised our ancestors from a long time ago." Micah's prophetic message of restoration was shame-shattering. Hang-on to this nugget, God's promises are forever true. He has not changed His mind about us... even in the middle of our mess-ups. Out of the depths of our mess-ups, He will give us a message. In the midst of our mistakes, He will give us miraculous opportunities for ministry.

I'm convinced that when I lifted my focus from the negative thoughts of being a pregnant teen, to the positive revelation that I was also pregnant with purpose and possibilities, my life shifted. Just like the woman at the well, dropping my pot transformed my life. Being affected by my situation was clearly understandable, but being defined by it was surely unacceptable; this would become my mantra. I was determined to shift my attitude from being defined by my circumstances, to becoming refined by them... made stronger, improved, and renewed. As a result of my attitude shift, my tested faith stirred up power as opposed to pity; thinking different led to living differently... living forward. My learning to live forward was not just about me, it was for those who would hear my testimony and begin to grasp hope for themselves. This would be the start of seeing the manifested (made apparent; noticeable) power of a renewed mind.

"God is able to take your life, with all of the heartache, all of the pain, all of the regret, all of the missed opportunities, and use you for His glory."
~Chuck Swindoll

Forget about what's happened; don't keep going over old
history. Be alert, be present. I'm about to do something brand-
new. It's bursting out! Don't you see it?
There it is! I'm making a road through the desert,
rivers in the badlands.
Isaiah 43:18-19(MSG)

Though we experience every kind of pressure, we're not
crushed. At times we don't know what to do, but quitting is not
an option.[a] 9 We are persecuted by others, but God has not
forsaken us. We may be knocked down, but not out. 10 We
continually share in the death of Jesus in our own bodies[b] so
that the resurrection life of Jesus will be revealed through our
humanity. 11 We consider living to mean that we are constantly
being handed over to death for Jesus' sake so that the life of
Jesus will be revealed through our humanity. 12 So, then, death
is at work in us but it releases life in you.
2 Corinthians 4:8-12 (TPT)

I forget about the things behind me and reach
out for the things ahead of me.
Philippians 3:13(CEB)

Cast your burden on the LORD [release it] and He
will sustain and uphold you;
Psalm 55:22(AMP)

Get rid of all bitterness, rage and anger, brawling and slander,
along with every form of malice. 32 Be kind and compassionate
to one another, forgiving each other,
just as in Christ God forgave you.
Ephesians 4:31-32 (NIV)

Make a list of the things inside your pot and also how long you have been carrying each one of them:

_____
_____
_____
_____
_____
_____

Now that you have confronted the things in your pot, how do you plan to defeat them and maintain your VICTORY status?

_____
_____
_____
_____
_____
_____
_____
_____
_____

*"We can never defeat it if
we never face it"!*

MY FREEDOM PRAYER

_____
_____
_____
_____
_____
_____
_____
_____
_____
_____
_____
_____
_____
_____
_____
_____

ASHAMED NO MORE
Free at last...Free at last

> *"Whatever you think about grows...
> Don't focus on what you are going through-
> focus on what you are going to!"*
> *~Dr. Caroline Leaf*

CHAPTER 6
A RENEWED MIND

When you hear the phrase "mind renewal," what do you think of? I firmly believe that mind renewal is the key to breaking free from shame. As Romans 12:2 teaches us, renewing our minds opens our eyes to transformation. A quote I once heard, "Eyes are useless when the mind is blind," resonates with me as I write this. When our minds are closed to the truth of God's promises and our authority as believers, admitting shame becomes a struggle. Though we cannot change what we are not willing to confess, and confession is a powerful tool for the soul. Brené Brown rightly says, "Shame hates it when we reach out and tell our story. When buried, it metastasizes." Confession liberates us from the grip of shame, empowering us to embrace our true identity.

"When sharing our story with someone who responds with empathy and understanding, shame can not survive,"
~Brene' Brown

<u>Words Follow Thoughts</u>

The words we speak have a significant part to play in mind renewal. With every word that we speak our future is listening. Whatever we think about, we will speak about. It is necessary to command our thoughts. Commanding our thoughts means to give our thoughts an authoritative order to get in line with the Word of God. Decide today to be intentional in your thinking. Think about and speak about what the Word says about you and not what your past says about you. Shame, fear, and guilt have the potential of distorting our self-perception and leaving us to wonder whether we truly have a purpose.

~~~~~~~~~~~~~~~~~~~~~~~~~~~~~~~~~~~~~~

"You cannot have a positive life and a negative mind."
~Joyce Meyer

The Shame Factor

The "shame factor" is an enemy-designed trap used to distract us from boldly stepping into our divine calling. The enemy uses shame to paint an illusion (in our mind) that we are what we did or we are what happened to us. The sad thing about this falsely painted illusion is that often times, we believe the lies. I am grateful to God for the truth of 2 Corinthians 5:17. I received the revelation that I am a new creation in Christ. The old me, my past, my mishaps, my misfortunes, my guilt, and my shame was wiped away by the blood of Jesus. I made a commitment to myself that I would not allow my past experience to conform me. I decided to allow the mind-renewing Word of God to transform me.

Exposing the Wounds

As I reflect on the healing process of my past heartbreaks and heartaches, I found that my ability to walk in the divine destiny that God designed for me required exposure. "Exposure of what" you might ask? **Exposure of my pain** and everything that had built a wall between me and my destiny. All of us, including the good, God-fearing, church-going, Christians have experienced emotional pain and shame. As for me, walking in pain and shame had become like quicksand, and it was pulling me down fast. As the eyes of my understanding were suddenly enlightened, I was compelled to uncover my wounds. Remember, we cannot conquer what we will not confront. According to John 8:32, it is TRUTH that sets us free. Therefore, in the spirit of truth, we must move from our history into our destiny. It is TIME!!

The wounds of my hidden shame and embarrassment were healed by the profound touch of Father God. His love, so powerful and all-encompassing, is instrumental in the shedding of shame. When we remove the mask and give Him 'surrendered permission' to touch us where it hurts, we will experience healing from the core. Shedding shame produces freedom. Oftentimes, we shy away from exposing our frailties due to a lack of trusting God. It seems that we trust in our ability to hide our pain more than we trust in God's ability to heal our pain. Psalms 147:3 says, 'He heals the wounds of every shattered heart, [curing their pains and their sorrows].' Hebrews 4:15 says that we do not have a high priest who cannot be touched by the very feelings of our infirmities. In other words, we can trust the Father with our wounds.

Once we uncover our scars and stand toe to toe with the truth of our shame, we give the Holy Spirit the freedom to clean our wounds. Once the infectious, cancerous area is cut away, the healing process can begin and freedom is near. Unmasking the pain shatters the lies of the enemy. The medicinal power of TRUTH breaks down shame to its core. Where the Spirit of the Lord is, there is freedom… there is liberty. Where the Spirit of the Lord is, shame is **completely crushed.**

Cast it Down… Cut it Away

Mind renewal requires a continuous effort. How we think can determine the trajectory of our life (good or bad). At any given time, unhealthy thoughts can and will find an opening into our consciousness. The Bible says (**2 Cor. 10:5**) that we must capture every lying thought like a prisoner of war and cast it out. An eviction notice comes to mind when I read this scripture. This is what I call a mind renewing strategy. If we desire to live in the freedom that Jesus sacrificed his life for, and rose from the grave for, mind renewal is crucial.

When I think of consistent mind renewal, my mind is drawn to caring for my rose garden. While attending to my rose bushes (on a daily basis), I search for leaves or anything that appears to be infectious. If I find leaves with black or yellowing spots, I immediately cut them away. The same process is necessary for mind renewal. Each time the enemy attempts to infuse our minds with negativity and infectious thoughts, we must cut them away. Use the Word of God as garden shears and cut down shame... including the roots!!!!!

~~~~~~~~~~~~~~~~~~~~~~~~~~~~~~~~~~~~~

Summing it all up, friends, I'd say you'll do best by filling your minds and meditating on things true, noble, reputable, authentic, compelling, gracious—the best, not the worst; the beautiful, not the ugly; things to praise, not things to curse. Put into practice what you learned from me, what you heard and saw and realized. Do that, and God, who makes everything work together, will work you into his most excellent harmonies.
Philippians 4:8-9 (MSG)

Do not conform to the pattern of this world, but be transformed by the renewing of your mind.
Romans 12:2 (NIV)

Then Jesus turned to the Jews who had claimed to believe in him. "If you stick with this, living out what I tell you, you are my disciples for sure. Then you will experience for yourselves the truth, and the truth will free you."
John 8:32 (MSG)

How many times have you replayed (in your head) conversations or situations that pained you?

_____
_____
_____
_____
_____
_____
_____
_____

Are you ready to uncover your wounds and allow the Lord to touch you where it hurts?

_____
_____
_____
_____
_____

What is your daily plan to renew your mind?

MY FREEDOM PRAYER

_____
_____
_____
_____
_____
_____
_____
_____
_____
_____
_____
_____
_____
_____

ASHAMED NO MORE
Free at last...Free at last

"The picture that we have of ourselves- our self-concept- will always determine how we respond to life."
~Myles Munroe

CHAPTER 7
YOUR TRUE IDENTITY

Our identity is incredibly valuable. According to consumer reports, identity theft occurs every two minutes. Due to the increasing number of these incidents, various corporations, banks, and financial organizations offer "identity theft protection." Almost every commercial, advertisement, and email stresses the importance of obtaining identity theft protection. While watching one of these promotional ads, I had an 'ah-ha' moment. I thought, 'Just as our physical identity can be attacked, our spiritual identity is also vulnerable. When we are unaware of God's Word, His promises, and His purpose for us, we leave our identity open to attack. How is this possible? The answer is the 'shame factor' – the feeling of unworthiness and guilt that separates us from God's love and purpose for us.'

The separation is not because He leaves us… it is because we move away from Him.

The Attack

As soon as we enter the world our identity is attacked. The sneak attack by the enemy comes forth because he is aware of something that we are not. He knows who we are before we know who we are… he knows that Psalms 8:5(TPT) says…"Yet what honor you have given to men, created only a little lower than Elohim, like kings and queens with glory and magnificence." This verse brings clarity to our ROYAL position; however, upon our entrance into the world, we are not aware of our "royal-ness". The early stage of vulnerability leaves us open for "the attack."

The enemy will make every attempt to attach all the weight of shame to our identity in hopes that we'll become unrecognizable to ourselves; he uses the weight of shame to mask our TRUE IDENTITY. This is a clear definition of identity theft… when one's true identity is hidden or stolen. I came to let you know that though you may have suffered mishaps and misfortunes, and those misfortunes and traumatic experiences were real, and they left some scars," **yes, you were affected, but not DEFINED.**

When you know in your knower who you are and whose you are, no devil in hell can hold you back. The only way to walk in the truth of our identity is to be **committed** to filling ourselves with the Word of God. I'm convinced that being committed to God, and His Word, has the power to change our life as well as the lives of those around us. So, remember this, whatever is feeding you is leading you.

The Word of God has the power to break chains, barriers, strongholds, and anything that rises up against His truth, but only when we do what it says. There is no stability in seeking to find our identity outside of the Word of God. The Bible says, "In the beginning was the Word, and the Word was with God, and the Word was God." The Word of God has and always will bring revelation to who we are (not our past, not our mistakes, and not our mishaps). Our true identity is in Christ Jesus and the message of the Cross. Be filled with the seed of the Word of God. I'll say it again, "whatever feeds us... leads us."

<u>Seeds of Greatness</u>

There are seeds of greatness and power underneath all of the rubble of your past. Your Heavenly Father is waiting for you to press into your God-given supernatural strength, and push forward to your designed assigned purpose. I'm confident that when we tap into the divine authority and power given by the Holy Spirit, a synergistic motion is created. It is with this power that we can plow pass the rubbish of our yesterday. I believe that in the plowing-through process, revelation of our purposeful existence, and the uniqueness of our creation comes alive... it's the season of enlightened understanding.

In the midst of uncovering the buried greatness within, it's essential to embrace the refining journey God takes us through. This process often involves removing layers of doubt, fear, and inadequacy that have settled over time. Just as a seed must push through the soil to reach the light, we, too, must navigate through obstacles and hardships to experience true growth. It's not always comfortable, but it is necessary.

When the eyes of our understanding is enlightened, we realize that the same power that raised Jesus from the dead is alive in us. Resurrection power is all we need to roll the stone of shame away. The devil will always try to use our past to break us, **but God** uses our past as resistance to strengthen us. As we press forward, becoming healed of our brokenness, we can impact the lives of many. We are valuable to God's Kingdom and greater days are ahead of us.

The full potential of your existence beckons you to rise up out of the shadows of your past. It is time to run to the light of God's purpose for your life and stop allowing your past to hold your present or your future hostage. Your Heavenly Father has not changed his mind about you, nor his plans for you. His gifts and callings are irrevocable. In the voice of a loving parent, I believe He is saying, "Rise up my child, your Kingdom assignment awaits you."

~~~~~~~~~~~~~~~~~~~~~~~~~~~~~~~~~~~~~~~

> *"When you know your worth,
> no one and no-thing
> can make you feel
> worthless."*
> **~Anonymous**

WHO AM I... I AM A QUEEN

My beauty... fearfully and wonderfully made.
I was created with a purpose...
a purpose that shall be fulfilled.
I have gifts and talents designed only for me,
and I will use them to make a difference in the world_
from sea to shining sea.
You see, there's no one like me... I am an original.

From the top of my head to the soles of my feet;
from the inside out, I am whole and complete...
Who am I? I am an original, and
I am a QUEEN.

I walk with my head held high in a spirit of dignity...
wearing a crown bejeweled with
isdom, knowledge, and integrity....
Never lowering my standards for anyone, you see...
I AM ROYALTY... I AM A QUEEN.

Though I have experienced misfortunes and mishaps in
my life, and I may have been knocked down
a time or two, but staying down
is what I refuse to do.

I'm not ashamed of where I'm from,
I've turned away from the wrong I've done,
now embracing the new creature I have become...
WHO AM I? I AM A QUEEN.

No longer imprisoned or entrapped by my past,
or opinions of negative people that pass.
Their words can't hold me, and their comments

can't mold me.
I now walk in my true identity.
An OVERCOMER I DO DECREE....

I choose to forget those things behind me
and press toward the mark of the things
ahead of me. The prize of a future filled with
HOPE and PROSPERITY...
WHO AM I????

I'm not a carbon copy of a great original...
I AM AN ORIGINAL... I AM A QUEEN!!!

~~~~~~~~~~~~~~~~~~~~~~~~~~~~~~~~~~~~

What are your takeaways from this chapter?

_____
_____
_____
_____
_____
_____
_____
_____
_____
_____
_____
_____
_____

What are your takeaways from this poem?

How have you allowed your past to shape your self image?

MY FREEDOM PRAYER

ASHAMED NO MORE
Free at last...Free at last

*"I found my worth...and my victory...
In His PRESENCE."
~RMJ*

Thank you for making me so wonderfully complex!
Your workmanship is marvelous...
Psalm139:14(NLT)

CHAPTER 8
KNOW YOUR WORTH

So, if the Son sets you free, you will be free indeed.
John 8:36 (NIV)

Are your victories predicated on the response of the crowd? Do you need the applause of people to affirm your place in life? Do you know your worth? Encouragement and applause have its place; however, it is out of place when allowed to define **our worth**. And it has no place when it comes to knowing **who you are** and **whose you are.** How we see ourselves determines the strength of the magnetism that draws us to our divine assigned destiny. Abba Father is the one who calls us victorious and more than conquerors.

God's Word says that we are victorious regardless of the opinions or voices of others. This is why we must be attentive to the words we listen to, and the words we speak. Jesus made it very clear that He only spoke what the Father said, and He only did what He saw the Father do. This was his example to us... Jesus set the standard for us!

Hope and Worth in Jesus

Jesus' victory came about through His obedience to the Father, and the same is for us. Our hope is in the promises of God as opposed to the voices of the crowd. Philippians 4:13 says, "We can do all things through Christ who strengthens us." When we say what His Word says, we can do what He says we can do. In the resurrected Christ, God leads us from place to place in one perpetual victory parade. We are victorious beyond the voices. We are valuable because were created in the image of the MOST VALUABLE ONE!

Worth is defined as the value of something measured by its qualities or by the esteem or value in which it is held. The qualities that we possess are found in God's Word, and the enemy doesn't want us to believe the "Word of God" nor does He want us to believe in the "God of the Word." He will make numerous attempts to rob us of our **value** and our **worth** by attacking our **FAITH** and our **IDENTITY**. If we waver or become unsteady in our belief that Jesus Christ is Lord, and He is who the Word says He is, it will be impossible for us to believe that we are who the Word says we are. In order for us to know our worth, we must know our **TRUE IDENTITY**! We must be confident in who we are and in the one who gave us our identification. In a bold stance of confidence, we can stand toe-toe with the enemy, and his lies, and not back done.

Many times we make the tragic mistake of trying to find our identity in worldly or earthly things… our titles, our personal connections, and our careers. When those things are gone or those seasons are over, we are left feeling as if we have no worth or value. It is time to recognize that our true identity is in Christ, our Savior; the one who has given us everlasting life. It is our Christ identity that connects us to our divine destiny.

When we understand our worth in Christ, we will not accept less than our appraised value. It is very important that we know in our knower that we are Royal and that's how he sees us... that's how we were created, and God has not changed His mind about His creation.

The Chosen Ones

1 Peter 2:9 says, "For you are a chosen people. You You are royal priests, a holy nation, God's very own possession. As a result, you can show others the goodness of God, for he called you out of the darkness into his wonderful light." It is God's Word that verifies and clarifies our worth...not our past... not the world... not what people think... not social media...

not the neighbors down the street... not your co-workers... It is God's word. You are not what happened to you;; you are not what you did. You are what God called you when He chose you. He called you whole, healed, delivered, redeemed... He called you **FREE**. No more shame holding you.

Your sense of sight should never override your FAITH. What you believe must be bigger than what you see! When you look in the mirror, the reflection staring back at you is not who you are. You are who the Father called you... Royalty. Even when there is no physical evidence of your royal status, just know that "Daddy-God" has not changed his mind about you. The Bible says, "When God chooses someone and graciously imparts gifts to him, they are never rescinded" (Romans 11:29 TPT). You have been chosen, and you have a royal inheritance.

Now, allow me to reiterate the previous statement or should I say "declaration"...your eye-sight should never override your FAITH. Place your trust in the Risen Savior. He is the one who has given us our worth. He has (past-tense) annihilated everything pertaining to death. He gifted us with an abundant life filled with benefits. Those benefits include HEALING, FREEDOM, PEACE, and JOY. Trusting in man-made/temporary things (titles, buildings, or denominations) are short-lived and can never grant us eternal benefits. Just as our worth is found in Christ Jesus, our trust should always abide there as well. He is the shame "Eradicator."

The Word of God is only one of our weapons. From time to time, during my personal Bible study, I personalize scripture; this is how I fight my battles. Allow me to share my paraphrased translation of Romans 6:12-14(MSG) and Galatians 5:1(TPT): "You

(**I**) must not give sin (**or shame**) a vote in the way you (**I**) conduct your(**my life**) lives. Don't give it the time of day. Don't even run little errands that are connected with that old way of life. Sin (**or shame**) can't tell you (**me**) how to live. After all, you're (**I'm**) not living under that old tyranny any longer. You're (**I'm**) living in the **<u>freedom</u>** of God. Now, let me be clear (devil), the Anointed One has set us (**Me**) free—not partially, but completely and wonderfully free! We (**I**) must always cherish this truth and (**I**) refuse to go back into the bondage of our (**My**) past."Wow… what a declaration! His word declares our royal position of freedom and victory.

Our value is rooted in the most valuable one of all, Christ Jesus. His shed blood broke the chains of shame (and all of its attachments) and made us worthy. There is nothing in our past that His blood did not cover. Now, it is time to intentionally contend for our victorious position of freedom, and walk in the fullness of our God-given purpose. I call it, "Living forward!"

~~~~~~~~~~~~~~~~~~~~~~~~~~~~~~~~~~~~~~~

"The value of your Creator should cause you to reconsider your own worth and value."
~T.D. Jakes

DEAR Shame,

I have an announcement to make. I've decided that you are not the boss of me. You no longer have a say-so in my life. I have allowed you to hold me hostage for far too long, and today I break free. I now understand how powerless you are and that there is no fetter that my faith in God cannot break. I will not be controlled by your lies or your fear tactics any longer. I will not be afraid to walk in my God-given designed assigned purpose.

You meant for the rejection, the mishaps, and the misfortunes to bury me in guilt and embarrassment; what you intended to harm me; God used it for my good. Your attempt to lure my focus from the prize ahead of me was intercepted by the blood of Jesus. He took all of my shortcomings to the cross. His righteousness became my new garment and His resurrection became my victory. I'm finally freed from the heaviness of your draining distractions. Your deceptive paralyzing taunts of fear, embarrassment, and guilt have been unveiled. I boldly stand in the blessed assurance that I am who God says I am, and I can do what He says I can do. I am fully equipped by the power of the Holy Spirit to fulfill the call of God on my life, and I am not ashamed to carry out the mission. What lies ahead of me is greater than what is behind me. It took me a while to grasp this revelation, but better late than never.

Today is the day that I am pressing forward... **UNASHAMED.** I realize that my pain produced passion, and passion has given me my platform. My mess gave me a message, and my misery is now my ministry. So, what I'm saying is, "The train of shame stops here." This is where you step off. Where the spirit of the Lord is, there is freedom; He who the Son sets free, is indeed free and that's what I am... **FREE.** No more shame holding me; VICTORY IS MINE. I am ashamed no more; free at last... free at last!

I refuse to be ashamed of sharing the wonderful message of God's liberating power unleashed in us through Christ! For I am thrilled to preach that everyone who believes is saved—the Jew first and then people everywhere!
Romans 1:16 (TPT)

Keep your eyes on *Jesus*, who both began and finished this race we're in. Study how he did it. Because he never lost sight of where he was headed—that exhilarating finish in and with God—he could put up with anything along the way: Cross, shame, whatever. And now he's *there*, in the place of honor, right alongside God. When you find yourselves flagging in your faith, go over that story again, item by item, that long litany of hostility he plowed through. *That* will shoot adrenaline into your souls!
Hebrews 12:2-3(MSG)

No matter what, I will continue to hope and passionately cling to Christ, so that he will be openly revealed through me before everyone's eyes so I will not be ashamed! In my life or in my death, Christ will be magnified in me.
Philippians 1:20 (TPT)

Now my beloved ones, I have saved these most important truths for last: Be supernaturally infused with strength through your life-union with the Lord Jesus. Stand victorious with the force[a] of his explosive power flowing in and through you. 11 Put on God's complete set of armor[b] provided for us, so that you will be protected as you fight against the evil strategies of the accuser![c] 12 Your hand-to-hand combat is not with human beings, but with the highest principalities and authorities operating in rebellion under the heavenly realms.[d] For they are a powerful class of demon-gods[e] and evil spirits that hold[f] this dark world in bondage. 13 Because of this, you must wear all the armor that God provides so you're protected as you confront the slanderer,[g] for you are destined for all things[h] and will rise victorious.
Ephesians 6:10-13 (TPT)

Now it is time to write your farewell letter to shame.

Dear Shame,

The thing that the enemy would try to use to bury me was the very thing that created passion within me. The pain of my past has become the passion of my present.
~RMJ

ASHAMED NO MORE
Free at last...Free at last

From Pain to Passion

From pain to passion, there's a road in between.
Some streets paved with potholes,
and things unforeseen.

Though the road has some detours that
lead to a prize, it's a prize I can't see
for the tears in my eyes. The thoughts in my head
saying, "God I'm so tired." But I press forth with
power gained from knowledge applied.

From pain to passion, so does this road mean,
climbing over my past, not stuck in between?
Does it mean to take lemons, and
make lemon-aid, with my gaze
on my destiny ahead-unafraid?

Unafraid of the missteps of my past close
behind; And the lies of the enemy trying
to hamper my climb.

My pain led to passion, and I say it means
that pain is the process that sits in between,
your purpose and promise,
your hopes and your dreams.
So trust in God's plans
believing greater to be seen.

Don't stop in the middle;
Press toward higher things.
Let your passion be birthed from
the pain in between.

~RMJ

The Fame of His Name

The Fame of His Name
breaks the chains and shatters shame.
It Heals the heart of hurt and pain.
I Love to call on that Great NAME...

Jesus, Jesus, that's the name.
The name that soothes the wounds, and brings
us shelter from the pouring rain.
I love to call on that great NAME.

The Fame of His Name...
It's where I run and there proclaim
Jehovah Raphe... Healer,
the one who reigns...
I love to call on that great NAME.
                    ~RMJ

Journal your takeaways from the previous poems:

I Am...

Created in God's likeness...
Ephesians 4:24

God's incredible work of art; His workmanship...
Ephesians 2:10

Totally and completely forgiven...
1 John 1:9

Spiritually alive...
Ephesians 2:5

A whole new person, with a whole new life...
2 Corinthians 5:17

The light of the world...
Matthew 5:14

Triumphant...
2 Corinthians 2:14

More than a conqueror...
Romans 8:37

Free...
John 8:36

I am, "Ashamed No More"!!!

JOURNAL

JOURNAL

JOURNAL

ABOUT THE AUTHOR

Renee Minor Johnson is an author and an ordained minister. Her God-given gifts of speaking, writing, and singing have presented her with opportunities to share the gospel of Jesus Christ in traditional and non-traditional settings. She believes that each gift and talent created by God should be used to glorify God and build His Kingdom. Through her testimony, love of Christ, and message of hope, she is committed to leading others to "greatness". As she shares the importance of knowing our worth and our true identity in Christ, her heart's desire is to see lives transformed.

Renee is married to Terry "Ranger" Johnson (27 yrs.). She and her husband stand side by side in ministry. Their tag-team approach, guided by the Holy Spirit, breathes life into their evangelistic ministry, ChampionsWithin Kingdom Builders. The foundational mission and message of ChampionsWithin is founded in

1 John 4:4, "Greater is He that is within us than he that is in the world." Renee and Terry are passionate about influencing and inspiring many to tap into the real champion within us... Jesus Christ. CWKB provides a "Lifeline of Hope" to various organizations (schools, universities, churches, etc.) from coast to coast.

Renee is a Rayville, LA native and is the youngest daughter of Pastor Willie Minor Jr. and Orleana Simmons Minor (both deceased). Renee and her husband, Terry, reside in Louisiana.

~~~~~~

Other books by Renee Minor Johnson are available @ Amazon, B & N, BAM, www.royaltyjrenee.com, and all retail booksellers.

REFERENCES

Note: The translations used for most scriptures are as marked; KJV used otherwise. (**The Holy Bible... AMP, CEV, ESV, GNT, CEB, GW, MSG, NIV, NLT, TLB, WEB, ERV, NASB, TPT**)

Healed Without Scars .... David G. Evans

Royalty/That's How He Sees Me....Renee M. Johnson

Drop the Weight

The Rebirth of an Eagle.........
https://www.youtube.com/watch?v=h8_T40WKSsw

Shame and Guilt .... New York, NY: Guilford Press Tangney, J. P., & Dearing, R. L. (2002)

Let It Go! .... Psychology Today

You Still Love Me .... Koryn Hawthorne

Why Guilt and Shame Carry A Strong Burden: This Is How To Make Peace With Them And Transform Your Life .... Tony Fahkry
Mission.org

www.ingramcontent.com/pod-product-compliance
Lightning Source LLC
Chambersburg PA
CBHW032129090426
42743CB00007B/524